KEEP FIT

Contents

Top Tips	page 2
Eat Well	page 4
Play Hard, Work Hard	page 8
Kill Those Germs	page 12
Sweet Dreams	page 14
Glossary	page 16

Written by John Townsend

Top Tips

In the pages of this book, you will find some top tips for keeping fit.

The tips are nothing magic. You just need a little effort to keep fit. Start gently!

Eat Well

milk for strong bones

nuts and eggs for energy

TIP Eat a good mix of different foods.

fish for brain power

bananas and greens for vitamins

Tuck into a cabbage if you can manage it!

5

Just say "no" to that large bag of crisps.

Too many fatty foods are not good for you.
Cut down on food that is bad for you.
Even a little change can be good.

Play Hard, Work Hard

TIP Keep your body in good shape.

Your body needs lots of energetic activity to keep fit.

Try jogging to the gym!

So try to run, jump, play and swim as much as you can.

Keep your body working hard all year. You can enjoy some activities even in the rain and snow.

Don't let the weather bother you. But try not to sledge over the edge of a ridge!

Kill Those Germs

TIP
Keep clean to keep fit.

Germs spread very quickly. They can make us sick.

Kill germs by keeping your hands clean ...

after using the toilet

after blowing your nose

after touching pets

when touching foods

13

Sweet Dreams

TIP Challenge the urge to stay up late!

Kids and grown-ups need sleep.

Enjoy plenty of sleep.

Sleep helps to keep your energy levels up.
So the message is:
Keep to your bedtime!

Glossary

energy	power or strength
germs	little living things that get in our bodies and make us sick
gym	where we can go to do sports and other activities
tips	good things to do
vitamins	things in food that are good for us